Apple Pie

by Kristina Porteous
illustrated by Nicole Rutten

Pre-Decodable 2

McGraw Hill Education

Bothell, WA • Chicago, IL • Columbus, OH • New York, NY

MHEonline.com

McGraw Hill Education

Send all inquiries to:
McGraw-Hill Education
8787 Orion Place
Columbus, OH 43240

ISBN: 978-0-02-145082-4
MHID: 0-02-145082-X

Printed in the United States of America.

7 8 9 LCR 25 24 23